WOMEN WARRIORS

HIDDEN IN HISTORY

Sarah Eason

CRABTREE
Publishing Company
www.crabtreebooks.com

Author: Sarah Eason

Editorial director: Kathy Middleton

Editors: Jennifer Sanderson, Ellen Rodger

Proofreaders: Jennifer Sanderson, Karissa Silvers

Design: Paul Myerscough and Jessica Moon

Cover design: Emma DeBanks and Jessica Moon

Illustrations: Jessica Moon

Photo research: Rachel Blount

Production coordinator and Prepress technician: Margaret Amy Salter

Print coordinator: Katherine Berti

Written, developed, and produced by Calcium

Photo Credits:

t=Top, c=Center, b=Bottom, l= Left, r=Right

Inside: Shutterstock: Alizada Studios: p. 17; Anton Ivanov: p. 41; Artyme83: p. 4; Sergei Bachlakov: p. 34; Angelina Bambina: p. 25b; Linda Marie Caldwell: p. 31; Combatcamerauk: p. 15t; Cris Foto: p. 45t; Vladyslav Danilin: p. 22b; Delcarmat: pp. 7, 13; Dptro: p. 25t; Formatoriginal: p. 15b; Giannimarchetti: p. 9; GoodStudio: p. 26; Martina Jarolinova: p. 11; Life in a pixel: p. 6b; Maziarz: p. 16; Daria Riabets: p. 45b; Jane Rix: p. 42b; Sergei25: pp. 32-33; Dan Shachar: p. 6t; Shan Shan: p. 21; Brigida Soriano: p. 12; Geoff Sperring: p. 42l; SueC: p. 28; Tanja-vashchuk: p. 30; Timaldo: p. 18b; Waldemar B: p. 22t; Andy Wasley: p. 18l; Xelbr: p. 10; Wikimedia Commons: pp. 37, 39; Frederick Forbes: p. 42t; Frederic Remington: p. 36r; Charles Marion Russell: p. 36l.

Library and Archives Canada Cataloguing in Publication

Title: Women warriors : hidden in history / Sarah Eason.
Names: Eason, Sarah, author.
Description: Series statement: Hidden history | Includes index.
Identifiers: Canadiana (print) 20200153285 | Canadiana (ebook) 20200153293 | ISBN 9780778773016 (hardcover) | ISBN 9780778773085 (softcover) | ISBN 9781427124791 (HTML)
Subjects: LCSH: Women soldiers—Biography—Juvenile literature. | LCSH: Women heroes—Biography—Juvenile literature. | LCSH: Women soldiers—History—Juvenile literature. | LCSH: Women heroes—History—Juvenile literature.
Classification: LCC UB416 .E27 2020 | DDC j355.0092/52—dc23

Library of Congress Cataloging-in-Publication Data

Names: Eason, Sarah, author.
Title: Women warriors : hidden in history / Sarah Eason.
Description: New York : Crabtree Publishing Company, 2020. | Series: Hidden history | Includes index.
Identifiers: LCCN 2019054373 (print) | LCCN 2019054374 (ebook) ISBN 9780778773016 (hardcover) | ISBN 9780778773085 (paperback) | ISBN 9781427124791 (ebook)
Subjects: LCSH: Women soldiers--Juvenile literature. | Women and war--Juvenile literature.
Classification: LCC UB416 .E27 2020 (print) | LCC UB416 (ebook) | DDC 355.0092/52--dc23
LC record available at https://lccn.loc.gov/2019054373
LC ebook record available at https://lccn.loc.gov/2019054374

Crabtree Publishing Company
www.crabtreebooks.com 1-800-387-7650

Printed in the U.S.A./022020/CG20200102

Published in Canada
Crabtree Publishing
616 Welland Ave.
St. Catharines, Ontario
L2M 5V6

Published in the United States
Crabtree Publishing
PMB 59051
350 Fifth Avenue, 59th Floor
New York, New York 10118

Published in the United Kingdom
Crabtree Publishing
Maritime House
Basin Road North, Hove
BN41 1WR

Published in Australia
Crabtree Publishing
Unit 3 - 5 Currumbin Court
Capalaba
QLD 4157

CONTENTS

CHAPTER 1

HISTORY'S HIDDEN HEROINES

In the ancient world and right through until modern times, most cultures have believed that war and fighting is just for men and not something that women should do. It is only in our recent history that it has become more accepted that women go to war and share the battlefield with men. We know that women have fought alongside men in recent wars such as the Afghanistan War (2001 to present) and the Syrian Civil War (2011 to present).

And we know that in World War II (1939 to 1945) brave Soviet female soldiers stood side by side with the men when their country was under attack. The Soviets even had brave female fighter pilots. These fearless women made daring nighttime raids on the Nazis. They were given the name the "night witches" because the enemy soldiers were so afraid of them! But what about earlier history?

In 2017, historians were surprised to discover that the remains of a Viking warrior they had long believed was a man was, in fact, a woman.

Digging up the Past

When we study ancient history we are mainly told that women had important roles, but as mothers and wives—certainly not as fighters. But is this all there is to it? If we dig a little deeper, the picture starts to look quite different. Although they were unusual, there were in fact some incredible female fighters and awesome warrior queens. These women were not content to stay at home and let the men do the fighting. They took up their weapons, went to war, and gave the men as good as they got!

Warriors Who Wowed!

We are now discovering that there were many real-life female fighters who wowed the ancient world with their bravery and skills. In fact, in some ancient burial sites, up to 37 percent of the dead warriors have been found to be female. So, how is it that these magnificent women are so little known? Why are so many of their stories not the stuff of legends, unlike those of male warriors? To answer these questions, we need to look at how history has been **recorded**.

The Scythian women rode and fought alongside the men. They lived between 900 and 200 B.C.E. Their skeletons have been found across eastern Europe.

HIDDEN HISTORY

Secrets Behind the Frontline

It wasn't only on the frontline that women fought in World War II. Brave female spies, such as the American Virginia Hall and the French/British spy Violette Reine Elizabeth Bushell, also saved many lives during the war.

So, Why Can't We Read All about It?

When human **civilization** first started to grow, between 40,000 B.C.E. and 5000 B.C.E., women in many cultures had great **status**. They were **priestesses**, they owned property and land, and they healed people with their knowledge of herbs. We can tell how important women were in these cultures by looking at the **artifacts** they left behind. There are a lot of statues of women shown as powerful goddesses and many images of women on other ancient objects.

Before 5000 B.C.E., 90 percent of all human statues were of women.

*In ancient cultures, the work that women did in their **communities** was seen as very important, such as grinding grain and other food preparation.*

Everything Changes

Historians think things started to change around 5000 B.C.E. as ancient civilizations began to grow bigger and more powerful. They wanted to take on more land and defeat the tribes around them. That needed brawn as much as brain! Men became seen as the powerful members of **society**, because they had the muscle-power to take on **rival** tribes. And women began to be sidelined. Around this time, artifacts showing powerful male warriors and gods became more common. And fewer and fewer powerful female images were created.

As society changed, images of powerful male figures, like this one of the great ancient Greek fighter Achilles, became more common.

Women–Why Write about Them?

As civilizations such as ancient Rome and ancient Greece developed, the voices of men were heard more than those of women. The roles that women had as wives and mothers were seen as less important than those of men, who were leaders, **politicians**, or members of the army. The ancient Romans and Greeks wrote down a lot of their history, but it was the men who were historians, and the history they recorded was mainly about men.

In other civilizations, such as the **Celts**, history was told through spoken stories, rather than written down. So if women did have more powerful roles in these cultures, we know little about them.

Historians Hunting Heroines

Today, modern historians are trying to find out more about women in the past. They are discovering who they were, what they did, and where they came from. And they are learning that in some **male-dominated** cultures, women broke free from their traditional roles in the home and went out to win wars! They are learning too that in other cultures, many women were very powerful and fought alongside the men.

As the truth about the past is dug up, amazing female characters are rising up from history, with astonishing stories to tell. Let's discover some of them!

CHAPTER 2

EPIC IN EUROPE

Europe's history is full of great warriors, from warring kings and brave knights to glorious military commanders. **Just as epic, though, were its awesome warrior women!**

Cynane, Super-Slayer of the Ancient Greeks

Alexander the Great was one of the greatest of all the Greek warrior kings. But have you heard of his half sister, Cynane? Turns out that his half sister was a sensational soldier in her own right.

Cynane was the daughter of King Philip II of **Macedon** and his first wife, the **Illyrian** Princess Audata. Audata raised her daughter in the Illyrian **tradition**, which trained girls in the arts of war. Cynane showed a talent for fighting and leadership. In fact, she was such a strong warrior that she became famous throughout Greece as a fighter to fear.

Cynane was born between 357 and 358 B.C.E. She came from a long line of great female Illyrian warriors who fought fiercely in battle.

Power to the Princess

Illyrian women were famously tough and often went to war, just like men. Cynane's mom wanted her daughter to be true to her roots, and just as tough. Cynane did not let her down. When she was just a teenager, Cynane rode out with the Macedonian army to take on another Illyrian queen, and fought her to the death.

When Alexander became king, he could see that his sister was a great soldier, so he took her with him to fight on the battlefield. But Cynane was becoming such a powerful fighter and army leader that Alexander started to get a little nervous—maybe Cynane might make an even greater ruler than himself!

Why do you think men like Alexander the Great have become so famous in history, while it is much more difficult to find out about women like Cynane?

HIDDEN HISTORY

Alexander the Not So Great!

Alexander was so worried about Cynane taking his throne that he had her husband Amyntos killed. He did this so that Amyntos could not help his wife become leader of Macedonia. Alexander then tried to make Cynane marry someone else, but this fearless female fighter refused. She decided to stay single, and concentrate on bringing up her daughter, Adea (who later became known as Eurydice).

Luckily for Cynane, Alexander was soon distracted by his next great military plan—conquering all of **Persia**. He soon set off with his army to defeat the Persians. With Alexander gone, Cynane wasted no time in teaching Adea how to be a fierce female warrior, just like herself. She taught her daughter all the great skills she herself had learned from her own mother: hunting, horse-riding, and fighting.

Cynane's Big Chance

In 323 B.C.E., Alexander died in Babylon. This was a turning point for Cynane—she knew it was her chance to seize power. However, with Alexander gone, his generals quickly tried to put his half brother, Arrhidaeus, on the throne. Arrhidaeus was believed to be "simple minded" and was not fit to rule. But he was a man, and Alexander's generals knew he could be easily controlled—unlike Cynane.

Babylon was a powerful city in the ancient world. It was filled with wonderful palaces and monuments, such as the stunning Ishtar Gate (below).

OLYMPIAS, THE POWER HUNGRY!

Another powerful woman was waiting to get her hands on Alexander's throne–Olympias. Olympias was the second wife (of seven) of Alexander's father, Philip II. She was also Alexander's mother. Olympias was not afraid to kill to get her way. She wanted to keep her power, and the throne for Alexander's baby son. Cynane knew Olympias wanted to get rid of her and Adea, so she watched to see what this ambitious queen's next move would be.

This statue shows Olympias with her baby son, Alexander. Olympias was fiercely protective of Alexander. In fact, she was so determined to get rid of any threat to him that she had even plotted to poison his half-brother, Arrhidaeus.

Determined to take control back from the generals, Cynane called upon her own army of soldiers to follow her and Adea to Babylon. There, Cynane planned to marry her daughter to Arrhidaeus. She knew that if she could achieve this, Adea would have control of the great army that Alexander had left behind—with Cynane right behind her.

Making a Move

The word quickly spread that Cynane was making a move on Babylon. Alexander's generals leaped into action. The chief general Perdiccas quickly sent one of his great commanders, Antipater, to meet Cynane on the way to Babylon, and defeat her.

Cynane was ready for battle. She fought Antipater at Strymon, and in a spectacular display of military might quickly won the battle. There was no stopping Cynane. Determined to carry out her plan, she sped on toward Babylon.

Friend or Foe?

Perdiccas knew he had to try to stop Cynane again—if she got to Babylon, it would be all over for him and his generals. Next, he sent out his brother, Alcetus, with Alexander's soldiers to take on Cynane. Perdiccas had a smart plan—he knew that Alcetus and Cynane had been companions when they were young. He hoped that Cynane would refuse to fight her old friend and go back home.

When Cynane met Alcetus on the battlefield, she was angry with him. She told her old friend that she couldn't believe he had turned on her—after all, he was her childhood companion. Cynane may have been hoping that Alcetus would be moved by her powerful speech and give up the fight. But she was wrong. Alcetus was determined to carry out his brother's wishes and defeat the powerful princess, friend or not. He drew his sword and killed Cynane in the middle of her speech.

Alexander, shown here on horseback with his soldiers, had trained his army to be a powerful fighting force. Alcetus knew that with Alexander's army behind him, he stood a chance of defeating Cynane.

A Twist in the Tale

When Alexander's soldiers saw Alcetus kill Cynane, they cried out in shock and horror. They could not believe that Alcetus had so **dishonorably** killed the great princess and the daughter of Philip II. They refused to follow Alcetus and instead turned on him and Perdiccas. The army demanded that Cynane's wish to have her daughter marry Arrhidaeus be carried out. Adea married Arrhidaeus and went on to become a great ruler and a powerful military leader, just like her mother. Although she had lost the battle, in the end, Cynane had won the war.

Sadly, Adea's rule came to a violent end in 317 B.C.E., when Olympias finally seized her chance to get rid of Cynane's daughter. She had Adea arrested and forced her to kill herself.

HIDDEN HISTORY

Hidden by Historians

Amazingly, Cynane's story was rarely told by historians through the centuries that followed her death. However, in more recent years, as interest in women of the past has grown, the tale of this powerful female warrior has come to light again. Today, Cynane is remembered for the powerful figure she was—one of the greatest female military commanders of the ancient world.

Boudica, Britain's Ultimate Warrior Queen

Few stories of women warriors are as well known as that of Boudica, the famous Celtic queen who took on the Romans and shook them to the core. Bold, brave, and utterly fearless, Boudica was the ultimate warrior queen.

Boudica was born around 30 C.E. in Britain. At that time, Britain was ruled by many different Celtic tribes, which each controlled a different area. In 43 C.E., the Romans began to **invade** Britain, and everything started to change. The Romans wanted to control the Celts and their lands and crushed any tribes that stood against them.

A Roman Wrong

Boudica married the king of a Celtic tribe called the Iceni. His name was Prasutagus. He had agreed with the Romans that he would divide his kingdom between his daughters and Rome's emperor, Nero. But when Prasutagus died, Rome demanded that all of the land be given to the **empire**.

Boudica was said to have a mane of long red hair that reached to her hips.

The Roman army was hated by many Celts because of its harsh treatment of them.

The Romans' Big Mistake

Boudica was angry at this action, and told the Romans she would not stand by and see her daughters' lands taken. So the Romans had Boudica publically whipped, and her daughters were punished too. Furious with the Romans, Boudica vowed that she would have revenge—and her great **rebellion** began. She raised an army of angry Celtic warriors and in 60 C.E. marched to take on the Romans.

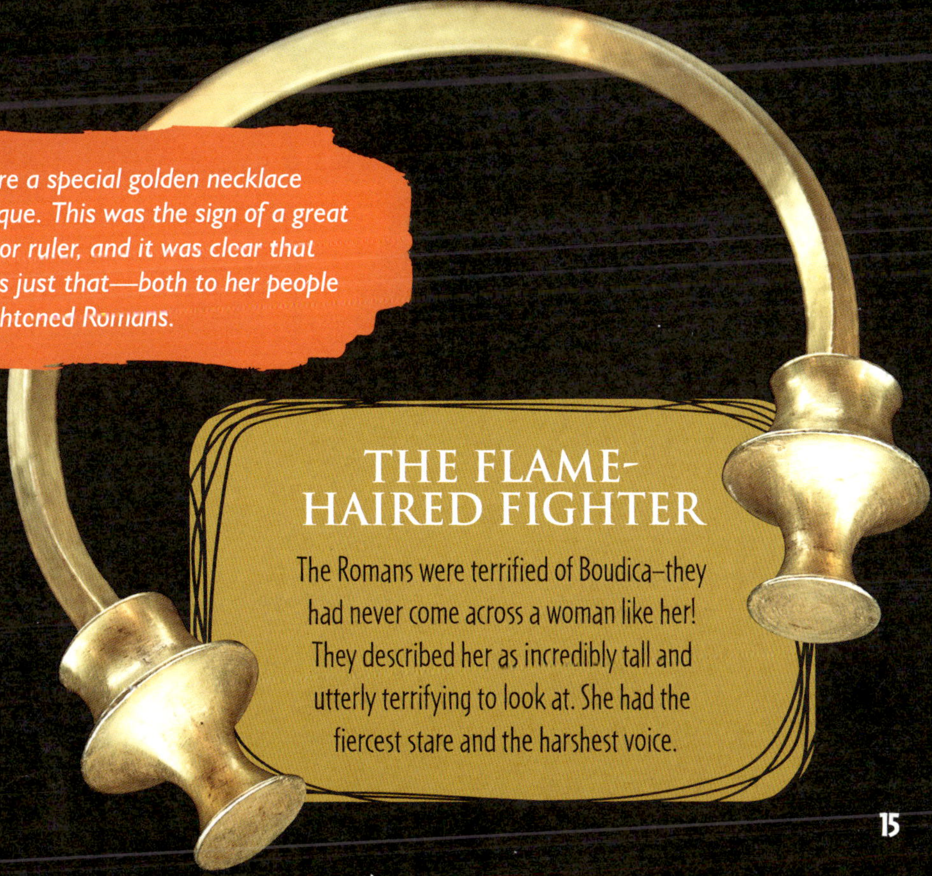

Boudica wore a special golden necklace called a torque. This was the sign of a great Celtic warrior ruler, and it was clear that Boudica was just that—both to her people and the frightened Romans.

THE FLAME-HAIRED FIGHTER

The Romans were terrified of Boudica–they had never come across a woman like her! They described her as incredibly tall and utterly terrifying to look at. She had the fiercest stare and the harshest voice.

Boudica Brings It!

First, Boudica hit the city of Camulodunum, which was a Roman **settlement**. She killed everyone inside the city and burned it to the ground. Even today, there are layers of burned earth beneath the city that are a mark of Boudica's devastating attack.

Next, Boudica marched straight for Londinium, which today is known as London. This too was a Roman **stronghold**, but when the Romans found out that Boudica was on the way, the Roman army **abandoned** the city and left everyone inside to fend for themselves. Rome's army knew that it was not strong enough to fight Boudica inside the city walls.

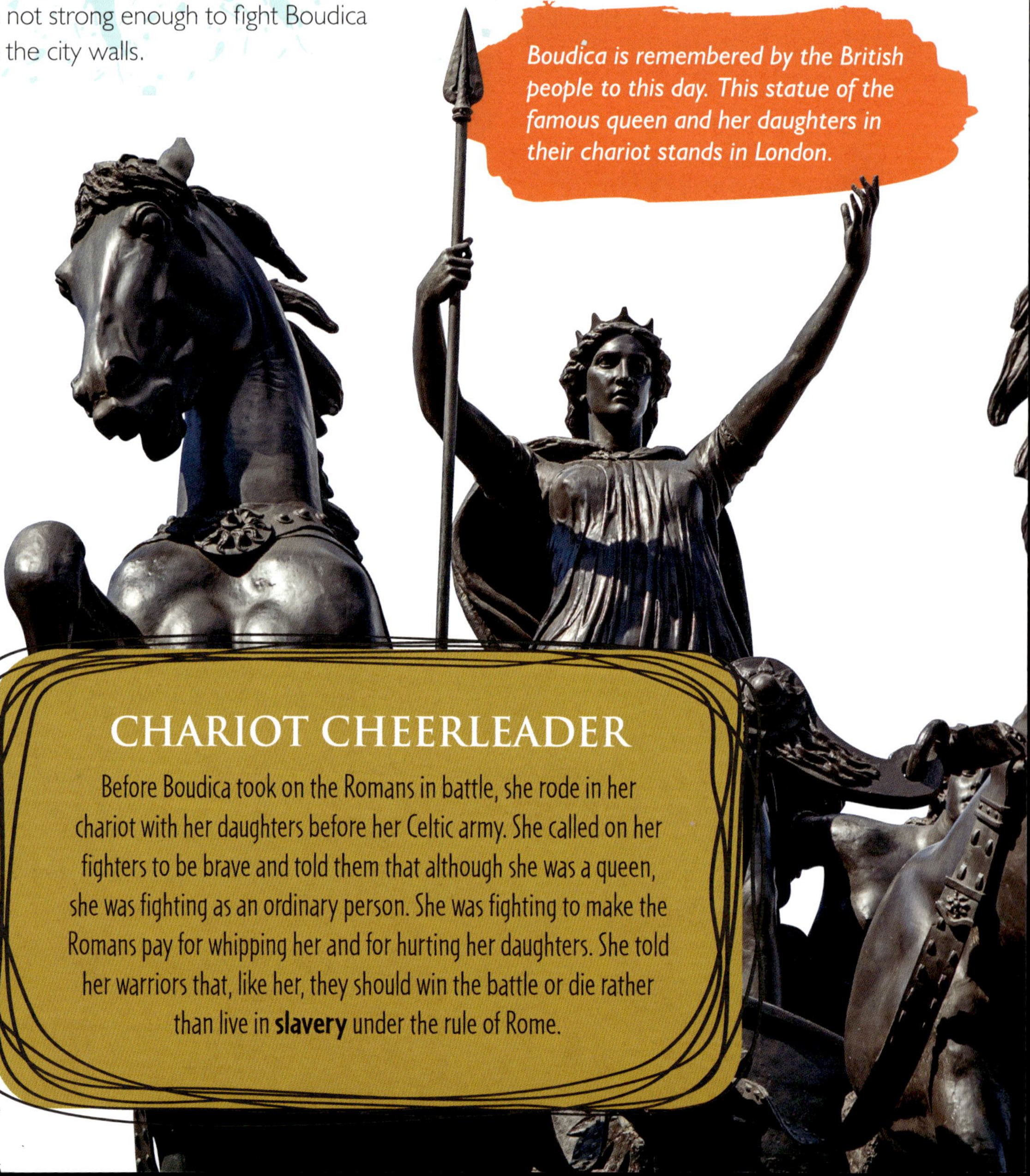

Boudica is remembered by the British people to this day. This statue of the famous queen and her daughters in their chariot stands in London.

CHARIOT CHEERLEADER

Before Boudica took on the Romans in battle, she rode in her chariot with her daughters before her Celtic army. She called on her fighters to be brave and told them that although she was a queen, she was fighting as an ordinary person. She was fighting to make the Romans pay for whipping her and for hurting her daughters. She told her warriors that, like her, they should win the battle or die rather than live in **slavery** under the rule of Rome.

*This is a reconstruction of a Celtic chariot. The Celts often rode into battle on chariots. One warrior would drive the chariot while another threw **javelins** at the enemy.*

No Stopping Boudica

It seemed that Boudica was unstoppable. Her Celtic army had grown, filled with Celts who had heard about her rebellion and wanted to join this fierce warrior queen as she took on the hated Romans. Emboldened by her great victories at Cumulodunum and Londinium, Boudica next headed for Verulanium, which was just north of Londinium. Just like her earlier attacks, she killed the people of the town and destroyed its buildings. By this time, Boudica and her Celtic army had killed around 80,000 Romans and showed no signs of slowing down.

Beaten by a Woman!

The Roman **governors** of Britain and the Roman army were in shock. They had been **humiliated** and their people had been murdered by the Celts, whom they considered **savages**. Even worse, they had been led by a woman! The Romans knew that to have any chance of stopping Boudica, they would need to plan the place of their battle with her carefully. They chose central England, near a Roman road called Watling Street. And Boudica and her army marched to meet them.

As the fighters gathered for the battle, the Celts vastly outnumbered the Romans. It must have seemed certain to Boudica and her army that they would win the day. But the Romans had chosen this place of battle thoughtfully.

This photograph shows Watling Street today. In Celtic times, the battlefield at Watling Street was narrow and surrounded by trees, so the Celts could not use their chariots to circle around the enemy and attack them.

The Celts often fought bare-chested and wearing little, if any, body armor. They believed that their gods would protect them in battle.

Boudica's Brave Stand

The Romans were positioned on a hill, so Boudica and her army had to march upward to meet them. The Romans launched javelins at the Celts as they made it up the hill, killing many of them before they got anywhere near the Roman army. Those that did were finished off by the short, sharp stabs of the Romans' deadly swords. Then the Romans attacked the Celts from behind too, killing thousands.
It was soon all over for the Celts.

Many Roman soldiers were terrified of the Celtic women who stood on the battlefield, waving their weapons and shouting at the enemy.

SUPER-SCARY FIGHTERS

Boudica is a famous Celtic warrior, but other Celtic women are known to have fought on the battlefield too. The Romans described them as almost as tall as the men and just as fierce.

But What Happened to Boudica?

No one knows for sure what happened to Boudica. Some stories say that she fled from the battlefield with her daughters, and they then poisoned themselves. Others say that Boudica died on the battlefield, fighting to the end with her Celtic warriors. One thing is certain, the flame-haired warrior queen was determined that she would not be taken alive back to Rome. Boudica's story ended at the Battle of Watling Street, but her legend lives on.

CHAPTER 3

AWESOME IN ASIA

Ancient Asia is famous for its great male military leaders. You may well have heard of Genghis Khan and you probably have read about the samurais. But I bet you don't know that some of ancient Asia's most marvelous military mights were women!

Fu, the Fighter

One of these great female fighters was Fu Hao. This amazing woman lived in ancient China between 1100 and 1200 B.C.E. She was one of the wives of Wu Ding, who was the king of a great ancient Chinese tribe called the Shang. During her marriage to Wu, Fu became respected not only as a wife and mother but also as an awesome army leader and a powerful politician.

Fu was incredibly unusual for her time. In ancient China, few women had anything to do with the army or ruling over people. But Fu was different. Her husband, Wu, trusted his wife so much that he put her in charge of his army of 13,000 men and named her Shang General!

Wu saw that Fu was super-smart and often asked her for advice when he needed to make important decisions. This was very unusual for men at the time.

We have learned about Fu from special writings the ancient Chinese carved into bones, like this one. They are called oracle bones.

Amazing Ambushes

Fearless Fu often rode out into battle herself, leading her army against nearby tribes that threatened the Shang, such as the Jiang, Tu, Ba, Yi, and Qiang tribes. When Fu led the fight against the Jiang, she took many of them prisoner. This fearless female warrior also **ambushed** the Ba tribe, taking them completely by surprise and carrying out one of the greatest military victories in Chinese history!

HIDDEN HISTORY

Tales from the Tomb

The tomb where Fu was buried around 1200 B.C.E. was discovered in 1976. **Archaeologists** were amazed by what they discovered in her tomb. It contained more than 100 weapons, including many battleaxes. In ancient China, only great military leaders were buried with weapons and other military artifacts. The hidden hoard of weapons shows that fearless Fu is clearly one of history's great heroines.

Trac and Nhi, Elephant-Riding Super Sisters

Trung Trac and Trung Nhi were two sisters who lived in Vietnam around 39 C.E. This amazing dynamic duo became known as the Trung Sisters and led their country to rebel against the Chinese lords who controlled it.

Freedom Fighters

At the time of the Trung Sisters, Vietnam was under the control of ancient China. The Chinese ruled the Vietnamese through tough laws and horrible punishments. Trung Trac's husband had been a lord in northern Vietnam and had been killed by a Chinese general for trying to overthrow the Chinese. When he died, Trung Trac and her sister took up the fight. They gathered an army of around 80,000 people. Most of them were women and even included the sisters' own mother!

The Trung Sisters famously set out on elephants to take on the Chinese. They trained 36 women to be their generals. What do you think this tells us about how these sisters viewed themselves and other women?

In 39 C.E., the Trung Sisters marched on the city of Lien Lau and sent its Chinese commander running for his life. The determined duo kept on with their fight, and within a year, they had gained control of 65 cities in northern Vietnam. They then announced themselves queens of a huge area of land from southern China to Vietnam. This was a step too far for the men of ancient China.

The Trung Sisters marched their army of rebels across the mountainous lands of northern Vietnam.

The Vietnamese are hugely proud of the Trung Sisters to this day. Many Vietnamese women see them as a ***symbol*** *of hope and courage.*

United in Death

The sisters had ruled over much of Vietnam for three years when the Chinese army fought back. It attacked the Trung Sisters and their army and defeated them in a number of brutal battles. The sisters had no choice but to flee. Crushed by the defeat of their **rebel** army, Trac and Nhi decided to take their own lives and drowned themselves in a river in 43 C.E. It was a sad end to a brave fight for freedom.

HIDDEN HISTORY

Early Women's Rights

Many historical accounts of life in ancient times paint a picture of women under the control of men, with little power to shape their own lives. Vietnam was unusual. Women in ancient Vietnam were respected in society and had a lot of freedom. Historians believe that the Trung Sisters felt that they were equal to their husbands and, for that reason, could take on the fight against the Chinese.

Lady Trieu, the Legend

After the defeat of the Trung sisters, Vietnam was once again under Chinese rule. The Vietnamese people were determined not to accept their fate, though, and one of their next most famous rebel fighters was Triêu Thi Trinh, better known as Lady Trieu.

Lady Trieu was born in 225 C.E. in a small Vietnamese village. Her parents died when she was just a toddler, so she was raised by her elder brother Trieu Quoc Dat. As she grew up, Lady Trieu could not bear to see her people so **downtrodden** by the Chinese, so she ran away into the countryside to set up a rebel army base. There, she trained thousands of people to fight. Lady Trieu began to fight the Chinese army when she was just 19 years old. By the time she was just 21 years old, she had fought more than 30 battles against the Chinese.

Legend has it that Lady Trieu was more than 9 feet (2.7 m) tall and rode into battle on an elephant, wearing golden armor and carrying a sword in each hand!

TRIEULY TOUGH!

Lady Trieu was tough through and through! When her brother tried to persuade Lady Trieu not to fight, she famously said, "I will not resign myself to the lot of women who bow their heads...I wish to...tame the waves, kill the sharks. I have no desire to take abuse."

The Chinese said it was easier to fight a tiger than it was to fight the lethal Lady Trieu.

The Legend Lives On

Despite Lady Trieu's brave attempts to overthrow the Chinese, her rebel army was defeated in 248 C.E. Lady Trieu despaired at her defeat—and threw herself into a river, where she drowned.

However, Lady Trieu's inspirational powers did not die with her. After her death, the Vietnamese people fought on against the Chinese, determined to continue the brave work of their fearless female fighter. Lady Trieu continues to inspire the people of Vietnam, and today she is seen as one of the country's greatest-ever heroines.

Tomoe, the Female Samurai

In 12th-century Japan, an amazing young woman became famous for her fierce fighting skills on the battlefield. Her name was Tomoe Gozen, and she lived in the age of the samurai, Japan's legendary fighters.

Tomoe was born at a time when Japan was caught up in a bloody war, with different **noble** families fighting each other for control of the government. Each tribe was led by a lord, who often had many wives or companions. Tomoe was the companion of one such lord, Kiso no Yoshinaka, who was head of the Minamoto tribe. Kiso fell in love with Tomoe and was so impressed by her amazing skills as a warrior that he made her the commander of his army.

Tomoe was famous for her strength and fighting skills. She was said to be worth 1,000 ordinary warriors.

Terrifying Tomoe!

Tomoe did not fail to make Kiso proud when he led his army into battle against his great enemy, the Taira. In just one month of fighting in 1181, Tomoe had cut off the heads of seven of Kiso's enemies!

Fighting to the End

Tomoe helped Kiso win many battles against the Taira, but their luck ran out in 1184 at the Battle of Uchide. Tomoe was one of just five of Kiso's fighters to survive the battle. Seeing that they could not possibly win, Kiso commanded Tomoe to leave the battlefield. But Tomoe was not ready to go down without a fight. She rode head-on into a group of Taira warriors and chopped off the head of one of their best fighters!

Story of the Samurai

Kiso was killed soon after the Battle of Uchide. No one knows for sure what happened to Tomoe after that, but the legend of this incredible samurai has lived on in Japanese stories, poems, art, and movies ever since.

Samurai warriors often wore masks into battle to frighten their enemies.

A HISTORY OF FIGHTING

Most fighting in ancient Japan was carried out by men, but women were trained to be warriors too. However, women were trained to fight only to protect themselves and their homes, not to fight in battles. Tomoe was special–she fought on the battlefield itself.

Zenobia, Desert Warrior Queen

The Roman army was a powerful fighting machine. Its soldiers were famed throughout the ancient world as almost impossible to defeat. But that didn't stop some awesome women from taking on the might of the Romans. One of these was Zenobia.

In 300 C.E., the Roman Empire was weakening. Although it still controlled large parts of the world, many of them were beginning to turn against Rome. One such place was the ancient city of Palmyra, which was ruled by the powerful and super-smart queen Zenobia.

At its height, the Roman army was the most powerful force on Earth. By 300 C.E., although it was not as great as it once had been, the army was still a force to be reckoned with.

Zenobia became famous throughout her lands, and the Roman Empire, as a fierce female fighter. She thought nothing of charging into battle at the head of her army to take on any enemy that stood against her.

Palmyra was in the middle of what is now Syria. It was an important place in which **trade** between the Middle Eastern countries and Europe took place. Its queen, Zenobia, was an intelligent woman who had been well educated by her family. Zenobia was married to Odanathus, a powerful man. He pretended to be loyal to Rome, but was secretly plotting to take complete control of Palmyra and the lands around it. Things took a turn when Odanathus was killed by a relative who wanted to take power for himself. And Zenobia saw her chance to take control of her kingdom.

Making Her Move

Zenobia declared herself **regent** of Palmyra, and announced that she would rule the **territory** for her son, Wahballat, who was still a boy. She killed anyone involved in the plot to kill Odanathus and told Rome that from now on, she would be ruling Palmyra.

THE SPORTY QUEEN

Zenobia was quite an athlete in her youth–and as a queen. She loved hunting, a sport that was seen as a hobby for kings, not queens. She refused to travel in a carriage, much preferring to ride her own horse, and she was just as happy to ride a camel!

Zenobia was said to have ***descended*** *from the famous Egyptian queen Cleopatra (right).*

Zenobia was on a roll. She quickly announced that what is now modern-day Syria and Turkey were separate from Rome, and under her rule. She then told Rome's emperor, Claudius Gothicus, that Palmyra was no longer under his control—and there was little he could do to stop her.

Fighting on Foot

After that, Zenobia put on her fighting gear and upped her fighting talk. She marched her army into Egypt, to take control of that country too. Zenobia amazed and impressed her soldiers by marching on foot for miles at the head of them, literally leading them into battle. The word about the feisty female fighter was spreading. And it soon seemed as if no one could challenge the mighty warrior queen.

EMPIRE BUILDING

At her most powerful, Zenobia ruled two of the biggest cities in the Roman Empire. She ruled over so much land that if she were alive today, she would have ruled over an area as big as Los Angeles and Chicago–and everything in between!

Things Change

Things were to change, however. In 270 C.E., a new Roman emperor, Lucius Domitius Aurelian, came to power—and like Zenobia, he was ambitious and a fighter. He was determined to take back lands that Rome had lost and wasted no time in ordering his army to march into what is now the Middle East. Aurelian drove his army right up to the walls of Palmyra.

This Queen's Not a Quitter!

Aurelian put Palmyra under **siege**, but still Zenobia refused to bow to him, and ordered her soldiers to fire arrows at the Romans below the city walls. She told her soldiers to get ready to fight—this queen was not about to quit! Zenobia told Aurelian that, like her ancestor Cleopatra, she would rather die than bow to the rule of Rome. This just made Aurelian even angrier, and he ordered his men to bring down the city no matter what.

Palmyra was once a magnificent ancient city. Sadly, much of its remains have been destroyed by a modern war—the Syrian Civil War.

As the siege of Palmyra got worse, the city quickly ran out of food. No one and nothing was allowed to enter or leave the city. The city that had once been full of riches and luxury became tattered and torn, and its people starving. Like her great city and its people, Zenobia suffered too.

Aurelian told the people of Palmyra that if they handed over their queen, they would be saved. Still the proud Palmyrans refused to give in. But Zenobia knew that her people could not take any more—to save them and keep her pride, she decided to run.

Riding across the Desert

Zenobia fled from Palmyra on a camel and raced across the desert toward Persia. However, the Romans sent troops after Zenobia to capture her. With their warrior queen captured and in chains, Palmyra surrendered to the Romans.

A Queen in Chains

It is said that Zenobia was taken back to Rome, weighted down by chains made of heavy gold and robes sewn with jewels. She was made to walk in front of Aurelian's chariot, humiliated in front of all of Rome. The famous desert warrior queen's brilliant rule had come to an end.

What Happened Next?

No one knows exactly what became of Zenobia after this. Some stories say that she took her own life. Others say that she lived out the rest of her days in Rome. What is certain is that she shook the foundations of the Roman Empire and made her mark as a warrior queen to be reckoned with.

LEADING THE WAY

Zenobia was a rare woman in history. She made the most of every bit of power that she had and tried to gain as much as she possibly could. In just a short time, this remarkable queen built an empire that threatened Rome itself. Zenobia's fearsome spirit and determination to live in freedom inspired many great female leaders in the centuries that followed her, including one of Russia's greatest warrior queens herself, Catherine the Great.

Even the famous palms that surrounded the city, and from which it got its name, were chopped down by the Romans.

CHAPTER 4

AMAZING IN AMERICA

The movies are full of brave male Indigenous warriors, riding into battle on horseback. Indigenous women are seen sewing, cooking, and tending to the children. But is that all they did?

Not Like in the Movies

Unlike the picture painted in the movies, in many Indigenous tribes, women had a lot of power. They made decisions on and helped govern their communities. Some Indigenous women even went a step farther—they were wives, mothers, and leaders, and they chose to be warriors.

SUPERHUMAN WOMEN!

We have learned of these extraordinary women warriors through storytelling and through the diaries and drawings made by Europeans who came into contact with the women. When they journeyed to North America, many European men were amazed to discover warrior women who fought fiercely for their tribes. Some European men were so frightened of these fierce female fighters that they even thought they had superhuman powers!

When most people think of Indigenous warriors, they imagine a man rather than a woman. Why do you think this might be?

Kwilqs, the Red Shirt Warrior

One such woman warrior was Kwilqs. She was a member of the Kalispel, or Pend Oreille people of what is now the state of Washington and southern British Columbia. She decided to live her life as a warrior rather than marrying. Kwilqs wore the red coat uniform of a British army soldier, which is how she got her name—Kwilqs means "red shirt."

Kwilqs was a great horsewoman and was known to be fearless in battle.

Kwilqs first became known to Europeans when Christian **missionaries** Pierre-Jean De Smet and Nicolas Point visited the American Northwest in 1841. They described their meetings with her in their journals, which is how modern Western historians have learned about this remarkable woman.

Riding into Battle

Kwilqs often led her tribe of warriors into battle. One account of her tells how she led a charge against a rival tribe called the Blackfoot. In another battle, she famously chased away a group of tough-talking male Crow warriors. When she returned to her camp, Kwilqs joked that she had thought the "big talkers" were men but that they hadn't been worth chasing after at all!

Despite her warring ways, Kwilqs lived to be an old woman and was greatly respected by her tribe as a warrior to be reckoned with.

Bíawacheeitchish, the Great Warrior

Another incredible woman warrior who lived around the same time as Kwilqs was Woman Chief of the Crows. She was born in 1806, into the A'aninin, or Clay people (Gros Ventre) of the western prairies. As a little girl, Woman Chief was called Pine Leaf. One day, when she was just 12 years old, Pine Leaf was kidnapped by a man from the Apsáalike, or Crow tribe, whose son had been recently killed. The man desperately missed his son and wanted another child to replace the one that he had lost, so he took Pine Leaf as his adopted daughter. He then raised her to be a great warrior.

Becoming a Woman Chief

As she grew older, Pine Leaf proved that she was a worthy fighter. In her first battle, she killed two Blackfoot men and then captured an entire herd of horses! As her victories in battle grew, she was honored by the Crow. They invited her to sit on the tribe's **council** and even made her their war chief. The tribe gave her the name Bíawacheeitchish, or "Woman Chief."

Married Life

The stories about Woman Chief are conflicting. Some say she married four women, gaining more prestige among the Crow. One story written by a man in his memoirs of life in the West claims she married him and made him a chief. Historians believe he was making his story up.

The Blackfoot (left) and Crow (right) tribes were often at war with one another.

This is a sketch of Pine Leaf. She was known to have developed battle plans and often led her warriors into war.

Leading Her People

Woman Chief lived among the Crow people as a war chief for more than 20 years. In 1854, she was killed by members of the A'aninin, or the White Clay people—to which she was born. She was visiting them to try to seek peace between them and the Crow.

Buffalo, the Brave

Another formidable Indigenous woman warrior was Buffalo Calf Road Woman. This Cheyenne fighter was famous for saving her brother and chief of the Cheyenne, Comes in Sight. He was wounded in 1876 at the Battle of the Rosebud. The battle took place in Montana, where the Cheyenne and the Lakota Sioux tribes were fighting against the Crow and Shoshone tribes, and their **allies**, the Americans. The Cheyenne people still call it the Battle Where the Girl Saved Her Brother.

Saving Her Brother

The Crow and Shoshone warriors shot the horse of Comes in Sight out from under him. The chief was also wounded and fell to the ground with his horse. His enemies were closing in on him when, seeing that her brother had been shot, Buffalo Calf Road Woman charged into the middle of the fighting and rescued him.

Stories about Buffalo Calf Road Woman riding into battle on her horse were told by the Cheyenne for many years after her brave act at the Battle of the Rosebud.

Winning the Day

Up to the point at which Chief Comes in Sight was shot, the Cheyenne were losing the battle. But Buffalo Calf Road Woman's brave act was so powerful that it inspired the rest of her tribe to turn the battle around, and win it.

Taking Down General Custer

Later that same year, Buffalo Calf Road Woman rode into battle with her husband, Black Coyote, at the Battle of the Little Bighorn. At this battle, the American army was led by the legendary Lieutenant Colonel George Custer. His status as a great war leader did not bother Buffalo, though—she is said to have struck the blow that knocked him from his horse before he died.

George Custer and his soldiers led many attacks on Indigenous villages before his famous "last stand" at Little Bighorn.

WARRIORS WRITTEN OUT OF HISTORY

During the 19th century, European **settlers** began to seek more land from Native Americans. As the American government argued about land with the Native Americans, they refused to let tribeswomen take part in the discussions. Many people believe that the settlers were terrified of these fearsome women and so "wrote them out of history" by refusing to acknowledge them.

CHAPTER 5

ACING IT IN AFRICA

Africa is home to a whole host of formidable women who gained fame for their fearless fighting. The continent has a history of amazing warriors and warrior queens.

The Amazing Amazons

The Dahomey Mino, or "Dahomey Amazons" were fearless frontline soldiers who fought for the Kingdom of Dahomey in West Africa, which is now called Benin. Their Amazon nickname comes from comparisons to women soldiers in ancient Greek myths. The kingdom these women served existed from 1625 to 1894 and was often threatened by rival tribes, as well as Europeans who came to Africa. The Dahomey Amazons stood up to them all.

Hangbe, Queen of the Amazons

In stories passed down about the Dahomey Amazon fighters, it is said that they were ruled over by a queen named Hangbe in the early 1700s. The queen's twin brother Akaba had been king before her, but had suddenly died. After his death, Hangbe took the crown.

The Dahomey Amazons were described by Europeans as great fighters who were strong, athletic, and battle-ready.

Hangbe is said to have ruled her kingdom for a short time, supported by her mighty female army. But her younger brother, Agaja, was hungry for power himself and believed that a woman could not rule. He forced Hangbe to give up the throne and took power for himself. He then wiped out any trace of Hangbe so that future people would never know there had been a warrior queen.

Today, the Dahomey Amazons are seen as great role models for the young women of Benin.

Fighting to the Death

The Amazons of the Dahomey became famous among Europeans for their great bravery. In one battle between the French and the fierce warriors in 1892, the women fought to the death. Just 17 of the 434 Amazonian women who went to fight in that battle came back alive.

HIDDEN HISTORY

Hiding Hangbe Away

Some historians say that there is not enough evidence to prove that Hangbe lived, but Benin women who claim they are descendants of Hangbe say that Agaja destroyed any evidence of the Amazonian queen to wipe her out of history.

Tough Training

Europeans who came to Africa in the 1800s noted the tough attitude of the Dahomey Amazons. They were in awe of these ferocious females. The women were just as tough with their training as they were with their fighting. One exercise was to climb a 393-foot (120 m) high acacia tree barefoot, without making a sound, even if the long thorns of the tree pierced the women's bare feet!

Tales of Terror

Seeing these awesome female fighters in action, the Europeans were amazed. They told stories about the legendary army of women and how they struck terror into the heart of their enemies. One story told how one warrior had brought back the skull of her king's enemy after she had killed him. She attached some horse hairs to the skull, and gave it to her king to use as a flyswatter!

She-Dong-Hong-Beh was the leader of the Dahomey Amazons in the 1850s.

The acacia tree is covered with long, sharp thorns. It must have been agony to climb one barefooted.

TOTAL RESPECT

The Dahomey Amazonian warriors were not allowed to have children or take part in ordinary family life–they were seen as married to the king. They were allowed to live in the king's palace and were highly respected by the people of the kingdom. In fact, each Amazon had a slave who walked in front of her, ringing a bell. The bell was to tell people that a warrior was nearby and to give way to her or look down as she passed as a sign of respect.

Battle Weapons

The Dahomey Amazons fought with round-headed clubs, which they used to batter their enemies. They also used **machetes**, and later, guns. Some of the women, known as Reapers, carried three-foot (1 m) long swords. They lifted the swords with both hands, and were said to be able to cut a man in two.

Role Models for the Modern World

In 1858, the then king of Dahomey, King Ghezo, officially made the Amazons part of his army. From then on, they fought with the men. Today, the Amazons are still as famous as ever.

The Europeans likened the Dahomey fighters to the Amazonian female fighters of ancient legend, and that is how they got their name.

Amanirenas, Killer Queen of the Kush

Amanirenas was a queen of the ancient African Kingdom of Kush. Kush was south of Egypt, in an area that now forms part of Sudan, in Africa. Amanirenas was born between 60 and 50 B.C.E. and ruled from around 40 B.C.E. to 10 B.C.E. She is famous for being a great warrior queen.

Here Come the Romans

At the time that Amanirenas was queen, the Roman Empire had stretched into northern Africa and was making its way toward the Kingdom of Kush. Under Amanirenas's husband King Teriteqas, the Kush fought back and hit Roman-controlled cities in southern Egypt. The battles lasted for five years, until Teriteqas was killed, leaving Amanirenas to take over the war.

Ancient images of Amanirenas show her as a huge, powerful woman, carrying weapons as she led her army into battle.

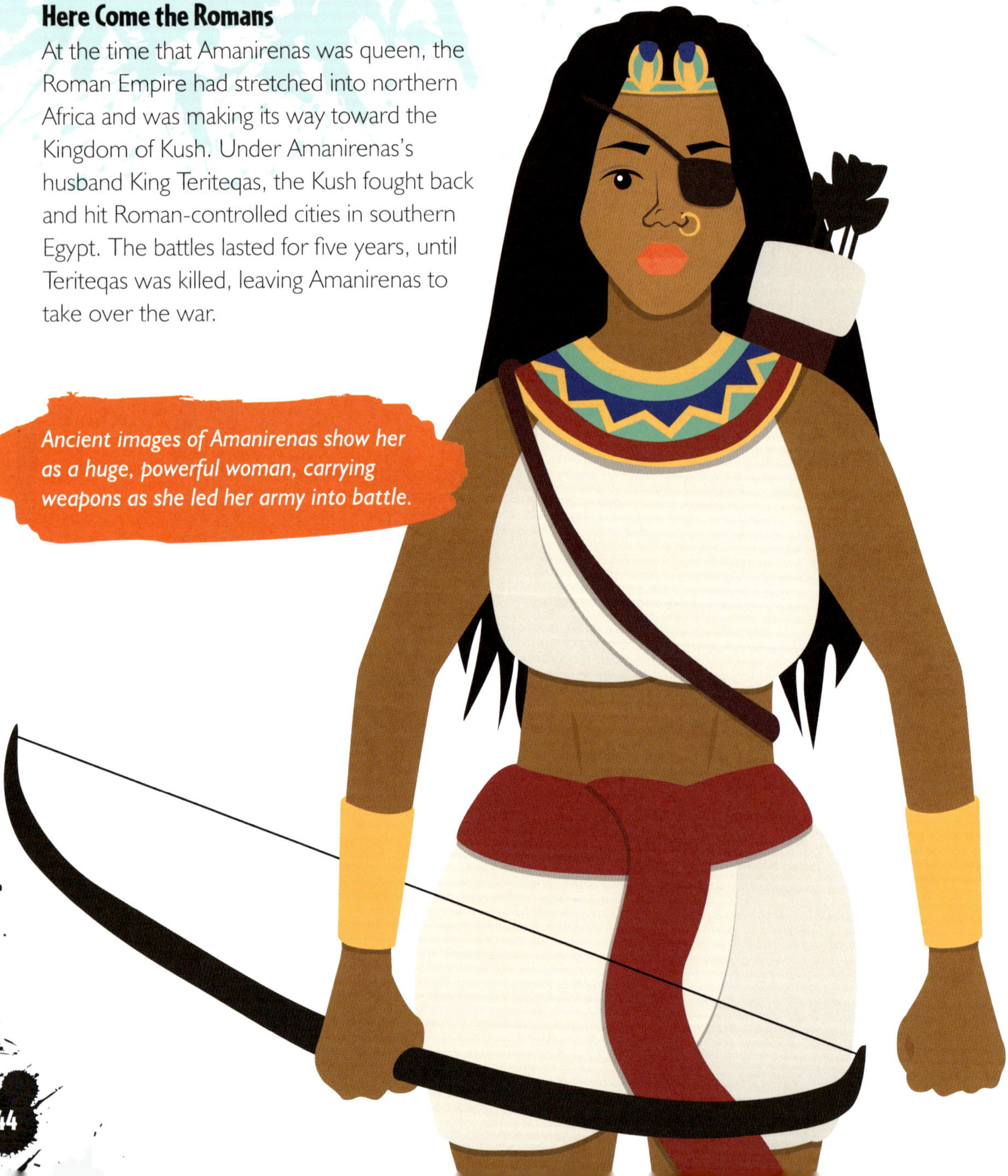

Angry Augustus

Amanirenas gathered her army and attacked the Romans. This made the Roman Emperor Augustus furious. He ordered his army to hit back hard, and the army tore through Kush, killing its people or taking them as slaves.

You Don't Scare Me!

The Romans harsh treatment of the Kush did not frighten Amanirenas, though. She carried on fighting the Romans and terrifying their soldiers. But the fearless queen was smart as well as a fighter. And after some time, she decided to use words as weapons. She asked to meet with the Roman emperor, to see if they could talk through their differences.

Give Up, Augustus!

Augustus was impressed by the boldness of Amanirenas. He knew that the weapon-wielding warrior queen would never give up her fight, so he decided to leave Kush alone. The queen of Kush had won the war and become a legend.

Amanirenas even had the head of a statue of Augustus cut off, to show what she thought of him!

HERE, KITTY, KITTY!

The Romans were terrified of Amanirenas, who fed Roman prisoners to her pet lion. And when the queen lost an eye during one battle with the Romans, even that didn't keep her from fighting on!

GLOSSARY

abandoned Gave up
allies Countries or people who help one another during wartime
ambushed Taken by surprise in battle
archaeologists People who examine buildings and objects left behind by people in the past to find out more about them
artifacts Objects from the past
Celts A group of European people that existed from around 750 B.C.E.
civilization An organized group of people
communities Groups of people who live and work together
council A group that meets to make decisions
cultures Large groups of people who share the same language and ideas
descended Came from, related to
dishonorably Without honor, to act badly
downtrodden Kept down
empire A large area of land controlled by one people and one ruler
governors People who make laws and control a place or organization
humiliated Made to feel very small
javelins Spear-like weapons
Illyrian Describes a group of tribespeople who lived in Western Europe around 1000 B.C.E.
invade To go into a country by force
Macedon A kingdom in ancient Greece that came into being around 700 B.C.E.
machetes Very large, sharp knifelike weapons
male-dominated Controlled by men
military commanders People in charge of armed forces
missionaries People who went to non-Christian countries to spread Christianity
Nazis The regime in power in Germany from 1933 to 1945, of which Adolf Hitler was leader
noble Describes a person who was not from the poorer part of society and who often mixed with kings and queens
Persia An ancient country that was in what is now Iran
politicians People who are involved in politics, or the running of a country
priestesses Women with religious power
rebel To go against something, or a person or group that is against something
rebellion A movement against something
recorded Written down
regent A person who rules for another person who is too young to become king or queen
rival A person that tries to defeat or be more succesful than another
savages People who have not become civilized
settlement A place where people have settled to live
settlers People who moved to a new country and began a new life there
siege A state in which a city is completely surrounded by an enemy and in which people cannot enter or leave that city
slavery A condition in which someone is held against their will and forced to work for another person
society A large group of people who live and work together in an organized way
Soviet Describes something that was part of the Soviet Union. Before 1991, the country that is today Russia was called the Soviet Union.
status The importance of someone
stronghold A place that is under the tight control of a group or an army
symbol Something that stands for or represents something else
territory An area of land
trade To exchange goods for other goods or money
tradition Something that has been done by a person or group of people for a very long time

LEARNING MORE

Read more about women who broke the rules and changed the world!

Books

Ancient Rome (DKfindout!). Dorling Kindersley Children's Books, 2016.

Anderson, Becca. *The Book of Awesome Women: Boundary Breakers, Freedom Fighters, Sheroes and Female Firsts*. Mango Publishing, 2017.

Charleyboy and Leatherdale. *#NotYourPrincess* (Voices of Native American Women). Annick Press, 2017.

Getting to Know the Native American Indian Tribes: US History for Kids (Children's American History). Baby Professor, 2017.

Pusch, Commey. *100 Great African Kings and Queens*. CreateSpace Publishing, 2014.

Websites

Find out more about the amazing Lady Trieu at:
https://amazingwomeninhistory.com/trieu-thi-trinh-the-vietnamese-joan-of-arc

Learn more about the fearless Trung Sisters and their amazing fight for freedom at:
www.britannica.com/topic/Trung-Sisters

Read more about brave Boudica and her rebellion against the Romans at:
https://kids.kiddle.co/Boudica

Find out more about great women warriors of the past at:
https://bit.ly/2sMQdWG

INDEX

ABOUT THE AUTHOR

Sarah Eason has written about science, geography, famous people, and history. She loves finding out about the past and the amazing people who lived long ago. In writing this book, she has discovered that there were many awesome women warriors in history, who all took on the world and showed them who was boss!